PRAISE FOR MELISSA BRODER

"Broder manages to conjure a psychic realm best
described as one part twisted funhouse and two parts
Catholic school, heavy on libido and with a dash of
magick. This gritty, cherry soda–black book . . . is
bizarrely sexy in its monstrousness."

—*Publishers Weekly*

"I don't know what a book is if not a latch to elsewhere,
and *Scarecrone* has pressed its skull against the hidden
door. It is neither drunk nor ecstatic to be here—it is a
state unto itself."

—*VICE*

"Lushly dark and infused with references to black magic,
Broder's work often feels less like a book and more like a
mystical text."

—*PAPER*

"Out to 'crucify boredom,' her poems show us how
any relationship with the divine is no less at risk of
engendering grotesque lust . . . What makes Broder
such a pleasure on the page is her insistence that these
dramas play out on a workaday stage infused with surreal
Pop and imaginative muscle . . ."

—*Publishers Weekly*

LAST
SEXT

LAST
SEXT

MELISSA BRODER

TIN HOUSE BOOKS / Portland, Oregon & Brooklyn, New York

Published by Tin House Books, Portland, Oregon, and Brooklyn, New York

Distributed by W. W. Norton & Company

Library of Congress Cataloging-in-Publication Data

Names: Broder, Melissa, author.
Title: Last sext / by Melissa Broder.
Description: First U.S. edition. | Portland : Tin House Books, [2016]
Identifiers: LCCN 2015041353 | ISBN 9781941040331
  (softcover : acid-free paper)
Classification: LCC PS3602.R6345 A6 2016 | DDC 811/.6—dc23
LC record available at http://lccn.loc.gov/2015041353

First US edition 2016
Printed in the USA
Interior design by Jakob Vala

www.tinhouse.com

CONTENTS

I AM ABOUT TO BE HAPPY

Can you feel it?

You are art and you are not art

Yesterday I thought it was good to be dead

I babbled, a wildwoman boiling your pelt

I wore you as my t-shirt and mouth

I said it was good for you to be art

Save me from death, let me rise from the dead

Today I bury your body

LUNAR SHATTERS

I came into the world a young man

Then I broke me off

Still the sea and clouds are pegasus colors

My heart is pegasus colors but to get there I must go back

Back to the time before I was a woman

Before I broke me off to make a flattened lap

And placed therein a young man

Where I myself could have dangled

And how I begged him enter there

My broken young man parts

And how I let the mystery collapse

With rugged young man puncture

And how I begged him turn me pegasus colors

And please to put a sunset there

And gone forever was my feeling snake

And its place dark letters

And me the softest of all

And me so skinless I could no longer be naked

And me I had to debanshee

And me I dressed myself

I made a poison suit

I darned it out of myths

Some of the myths were beautiful

Some turned ugly in the making

The myth of the slender girl

The myth of the fat one

The myth of rescue

The myth of young men

The myth of the hair in their eyes

The myth of how beauty would save them

The myth of me and who I must become

The myth of what I am not

And the horses who are no myth

How they do not need to turn pegasus

They are winged in their unmyth

They holy up the ground

I must holy up the ground

I sanctify the ground and say fuck it

I say fuck it in a way that does not invite death

I say fuck it and fall down no new holes

And I ride an unwinged horse

And I unbecome myself

And I strip my poison suit

And wear my crown of fuck its

MY OWN NOTHING

I went under my skin

Which was my old skin

And under the skin of my soul

Which was an old soul

Though new to me

There was so much silence

I was surprised to like it

I saw that all my wounds were only dust

And when I turned to dust they would be vanished

And saw that I would have to be the mother

I have to be the tit and friend and child

And stroke my hairs and say peace

The hairs on my head and the hairs on my soul

They are bulbing in the rain

They look like crops and I am scared of them

Because one day they will be dust

And silence knows they will be dust

But what will become of silence

When everything else dusts

I have to know the silence will hold on to me

Know it not by head or by reflection

But touch it in the emptiness beneath my dust

Already returning me to light

COSMIC DITCH

I can't believe how much the darkness

Light is all the time but I see wrong

Will you be ok? asks the old god

You will be ok, says the new god

O I've been so darkness since the old god left

I've been purple incense

This is the shittiest part of the universe

Maybe it's the best

Tell me how to feel and I will feel it

Make me into a socket

I want to bleed electricity on the shadow of the world

I want to be zero

KILLER RESCUE

I don't glow nothing enough for this life

Or I need to glow more than the other nothings

Or my holes are tombier and more instant

They resurrect starving with or without fuxx

I keep eating opals trying to get over

The opals look like lost light but they only spook my holes

Send in a moon drone to whisk my whole thing off

Take me to sky castle

GLOWING LOSER

Neon coming from outside me cursed be

Light from the most high I want you

Ditches in my head I fall in every dawn

The bad soldiers in there want me corpsed

I am sorry soldiers

Get on your knees and become women

Become my women

Worship light and in doing so transform

Do not ask me how

Something has to do it for you

Something higher or other

An inner other

A sky in there

The good sky

Fall on your swords

Don't die

Become other

See you as the sky sees you

See me that way too

BONE ROOMS

Ladder to the genitals of god

You never go high enough

I guess the skull must have its purpose

Mine might even give me silence

Mostly I am full of names

Demetrius and Christopher and Daniel and John

Cemeteries built around those letters

I dig the dead boys up and try to dance

In my bedroom I am dancing with skeletons

A cotillion of cartilage and the meat of my life

I will let the meat rot for a pile of teeth

The world should forget me I am animating clavicles

Now I'm in the kitchen brining hip bones

There are femurs insulating all the walls

I am ribbing up the windows of the real

I am never getting over my mind

IN WANT OF RESCUE FROM THE REAL

My mindfriends went

They offed themselves

I made new mindfriends fast and wet

But they kept dying dry

Fantasies die so dry

Still I held on

Because the real is arctic

And I am without womb

And the char of inner Earth

Will ash my bones sometime

Then they all began to die

Before they even breathed

And I could see their corpses

Before I saw their eyes

And a thousand past-life deaths

Tore the mask off my mind

And I am scared of death

And I am scared of life

NECRO GLOW

Wreck my temporary wrists in the white of the sun

The sun says it is happiness but I get colder

And everything becomes a stairway to a hospital

And I from self to nature back to self

And dark is the dark of having to be a body

Daylife in the boneyard not my own

The cruel of the mind in the sack of the having to die

The sunlight laughing in my face because it knows

And everything goes tone-deaf when it is born

Deaf to the howls of the other side

Blind to the sane of the dead and dying

Sand on the mirror from my last life

Go there honey go under the ground

I who never wished to be free

I see freedom and I am mourning

The shadows of boys in the sun

They are forever and I am melting

Maybe I can be here just this once

Maybe I can eat the part that is dying

Maybe I'll shit out the minutes

I have been waiting to be split open

I wait for words from the other side

Wings should reveal themselves big and kind

Everyone is crying really hard

MAN'S SEARCH FOR MEANING

There is a lot of love and then there isn't

Then there is

I look to the shitdoors for love

Because they glitter

O the glittery shit

So much more magnetic than what

I have inside me

Inside me is more shit

But not glittery

Though below the shit is maybe a fucking temple

And when one shitdoor closes

You must build another shitdoor

From the dregs of reality and shitmind

O bless those dregs

With fantasy and therein

Lies your glitter

Yes, bless that glittery shitdoor

So much like the first door

But this door will be different really

Infinite shitdoors if you want them really

I want them

WHAT WE LOVE MOST IS DEFINITELY GOING TO KILL US HALLELUJAH

Wade in the water

Wade in the goddamn water

I have been wading

I wade and wade and don't even know

The water dissolves me

The soothing water

The water as mother

The water is burning

I am ready to burn

I am burning me up

Every day I burn and burn

Every day I lose the wade

I listen for the water

I cannot tell me the water

Words never in or of the water

They are dancing around it

They are pointing to the water

I am pointing to the water

I say *look look water!*

I say *where?*

TEARDROP PERFUME

Definitely puke my heart up on the green grass

The whole ground lifts and flips me into you, but you're

    not there

Men without homes are farting behind me

The grass is their home, why can't I be them?

There is a kind of love contingent upon nothing

I'm afraid to be serene for it

I'm still hooked on plastic clocks

Make them disappear

AMERICANS

Clocks are all that are coming to me
Better laugh back into childhood feeling
Before it is too gone
Yes I see a pink ocean overtake the clocks
Yes it is only a hallucination
And I don't know if the ocean has feelings for me
But the shadow of a boy keeps me safe
From me
Though the shadow
Is actually me
And when a warplane flies over the waves
I don't remember god
And when my childhood feeling surfaces
I kiss the shadow of my boyself
And eat sand

BIRTH CURTAIN

I am such a cut cock

Bless your mother never cutting your cock

You are what it looks like to be real

What did I look like when I was real?

I vow to never go there again

To the land of the silent faeries

They were singing but I couldn't hear

I'm unreal now but still can't hear

The faeries judge me for my fantasies

They should have saved me from the real

I see other people's trashdreams

My fantasies are so pure

Once I never kissed an uncut cock before

Now I see yours flying around the room

You should uncut vomit for me

I want to touch your back and feel you burping

Fly around the room on your uncut puke

The room is black and in my ears

Faeries keep calling me

I can be deaf and they're still here

LIKE A REAL FLAME

I want the hole in my ear to be quiet

And inside the hole in my ear to be quiet

And I want it to tell me what to do

Or I will go to my lover's mouth

And say *oh my quiet*

I am coming

And tell the quiet how its kingdom should be made

Though the quiet has already eaten me

Because the quiet loves me

But does the lover love me

And why must the quiet be so quiet

And why can't the quiet have a cock

And where is its violet mouth

Its ten fingers with which to fix me

And where is its belly breathing

And O I want to be fixed

But I am already fixed

Why don't I feel it

BORING ANGEL

Now I know the trick is fantasy

I always knew it

But I didn't know the problem of bodies

Or I didn't know it entirely

How you must abandon the bones of the real

No angel wings projected on the ribcage

I had bloodstained sheets and I could not let go

I noosed myself on them in the woods

And hung there for eighteen days

Until I myself became an angel

Now I make love with no body

I do it with my halo chanting

Set me alive and fucking

A boy attached to no reality

He who needs no milk or punishing

He who will never abandon

How I love my celestial being

He who will never corpse

We are only air my seraphboy and me

Fucking with no eyes and flying

I LOVE WRONG

I am a monster with zeros in his gut
Who wants a doll made of flesh
To hold between two claws
And stroke its body, become a vow
A vow to the flesh of the doll
Never to myself or god
Or monster mother watching over
How easy making vows to a doll
So easy to see it as holy
Through my sad monster eyes
That no one likes the look of
I have always wanted something holy
To vanish the buzz in my forehead
My skull has silence but never enough
The world has never provided
I project a spirit in the doll
It speaks a great silence
It speaks my childhood dreams
I write them for its tongue

I write myself a new end

Where I am buried by the doll

And candles lit around my grave

As though I had actually lived

CESAREAN

At dawn they slit the nerve

Which connects me to a perfect place of darkness

Inside a giant husk

And they take me to its thighs

And lay me on the wintery thigh of this giant husk

Where inside it was summer

And all day long I beg to be let back in

I do this by living

I grow a rash of blood

And see things with my eyes

I see a flag on the thigh of the husk

It says *quick and painless*

I see an ocean almost like my husk

But it is not the same

My husk had a mellow sea

This one is frozen all the time

Even when the winter sun is blazing hot

They dress me up in beautiful robes

And quiet me up with cocks

And teach me how to vomit

Until I go mistaking pleasure for joy

And forget the husk completely

LIVING VOMIT

Sick people find each other and it is not a good thing

Sometimes it is a great thing

Every person is a sick person

Is that even true?

I lap your milk of illness up

It nurtures my dying

How bad am I doctor?

Very fatal, getting final

SAFE BLADE

In my sickness I was whole tit

Now I must suck ether

Which is the stars and where I am meant

I never knew I'd miss the flesh

And do I miss the flesh or the fake heat

That glinted off the sword I gripped

Which kept me safe from me and my disease of more

Though sword and heat were also the disease

The sword I slung at man's plasmic heaven

Applauded by the hands of dead but not their spirits

Spirits are you with me now although I cannot see

Sickly still in my lust for ashes

INNOCENT GROUND

Smeared in violent lipstick

A day with no boy in it

I don't touch reality

But I'm on the map of want

And here I am here I am

Jewbag plus some evil

And I dream you and I dream you

Eyefucks in the blanket

SKELETON GLITTER

The creepers are of the brain variety

The creepers are all me

Creep on me

Hello god

Why can't I be good

Shadow of the baby

Redemption of the soft friend

She said she would never

Leaving me

I walk through the wrong door

Pressed head and nothing is enough

I am looking for ways to get out

I am investigating

And I do remember the sky

I remember living up

If only I was blanked

The ground would give me a hug

Come in and wolf me

Enter the chambers and be them

Shipwreck and bathe in blank

We are talking serious baptism

And I know where not to go

And I know where not to go

And I run right to that place

And it's gleaming

INSTANT RAIN

Fall in all the wells at the same time

Yes I think I am having a human experience

I died in the mind

I died today

The blue sun in the blue sky like my face

My face could never hide anything

I went under my face and found curtains

I played a girl

LIQUID END

What you get is emptier

What you do is throw it all away

The lamb's blood on the door

Pestilence summer

Still your fingers smell of darkness

The darkness opens new holes

Let there be ditches

Let you die in ditches and never use again the body of
    another

The bruises you shall take with you and heal next life

Last life you were a locust

Last life you were a person

Ghosts of make-believe gods hanging around the television

No housecats

Jew of the salt and salty tastebuds

When your mother's hair falls out you will know

Roses weep for your future knowing

Find bones beneath the poolhouse of the world

The poolhouse indicates the pool is elsewhere

It is nearby but not on this planet

The bones are of god's dreampeople

The dreampeople are us

We are the ones who are supposed to be better

Something broke inside

Something was broken at conception

Now god fills with guilt

Now god cries for all of us

There is no punishment

Just the mother of suicide child

God wants to throw the stars back in the cauldron

Put down the receiver and start again

THE VANISHING WOMAN

I was afraid to become nothing

When all I ever wanted was vanishing

You can really be anything

Especially dead, which is a prayer

Though I do not know my soul yet

I think it is made of medicine

I have to believe my soul is everything

And all on Earth is just a mood

And now I am a woman who is helping me

And now I am the ocean hallucinating me

Face of blinks and grave of flesh

My soul just floating around them

SALT

How can you go swimming in another human being?

I am swimming and asking for light

Once I paddled into dust and fucking

And the horsemen and ruin

And the poisonous hollows of a projected blue eye

And cracked my skull on all and caught more disease

In my already dreadmind and entered the medicines

Of no human power, the forests of disappearing moans

Which were rich in sap but lacked dissolve

Fertilized against my own swimming nature, Aleph

I am swimming for you now and I don't care

When you leave the forest you do not become the ocean

And I have become the desert trying to swim in the ocean

And knowing this, carrying the forest floor in a sweet
    wood coffin

And the blackbrush and rocks, the yucca and cacti of
    receded oceans

Which were never oceans at all or there would have been
    shells on the sand

They only looked like oceans in my thirst, I cut the old
   horizon
With a sword you have given and I gut the heavens
And bleed their light and swim in that

SENSATION OF IS

Horses in the night take me away from me and I am glad

In the morning my demon kingdom come again

Demon me demon head demon not enough and never
    enough

The trauma of this living is that it is real

Oh and then my casket lowers into the ground

And after that a navy sky and me alone in it

Me alone again with the stars

Me back to the blaze of ink the first one

Me just a tadpole and also made of everything

Like in the beginning and I remember all of it

The first forgetting how at birth they took me far from me

And how I was not glad to be taken

And I am told to stop thinking about dying

Ok fine then nothing

MOLD HEAD

Pray to me from inside the blister, which is your own blister
Your personal hood of hell and everybody's
I believe we eat the same fruit, ultimately
Though when we see our own reflections in the water of
　　our blisters
We pull the skin up over our eyes and say *aren't I different*
Aren't I different aren't I
But the water is the same
And the gaze is the same
If you know how to look through the all-seeing eye
Have you gone down to the sperm code?
Have you licked up your mammal sauce?
It is in the rabbis' sways
And in the priests it fires incense
Glitter of the infinite to choke you in a blissful way
Eternal silence, my little blood cerebrum
Millions of mouths flap to someday fuck the quiet
I have no time to pray

DUST MOAN

A love that should not exist on earth

I am in the wrong love or on the wrong planet

I am already heaven or maybe illusion

Can people tell how mirage I am?

How is love supposed to look and feel?

I half-ask god but am scared to hear

Hide the seams of prism children I am

So I do not have to kill them all

SPACE ORPHAN

When I get the shakes they spell M-O-T-H-E-R

I fill the world with blank vomit that I spew in blank

Sorry for the first tit in my mouth that didn't milk

Sorry I'm not yet the stars and in skin

A slum until the end I call it body

When ruin comes I'll hug me briefly

Then I'll dance around an astral fire in my skull

Then my bones will turn to silence I can't wait

ARE WE FEAR

The sky told me nothing about myself
The stars told me nothing about myself
Jupiter gave me zero
Except that I am dust
Which is a lot to go on
But not enough to stop the death
Where are we going to live?
I said to my unknown self
When one of us is dead
She did not say
But opened up a curtain
Where her silence lived
And I went behind the curtain
And laid my skeleton down
I lay in silence as she stroked my tired head
And then I heard a roaring crowd
And knew that I had been onstage
And knew that I was good

BROKEN OCEAN

But then the water grows dark and recedes

I guess it is self-protection

To imagine the part where the water grows dark and recedes

As everything grows dark and recedes

I guess

I need a jumping-off point to this image

Love is the jumping-off point to this image

But love isn't even the water

Real love is the light

Don't you know that yet?

The water is something else

As anything that grows dark and recedes

Is something else not love

Fine then I don't want love

Fine then I don't want love

I want the water

TASTE TOMBS

My death is god's, how will it salt me?

Final sunburn or the gag of candy

My hair is god's and when it goes to dust

The worms will bone their ghostdicks in my scalp

And I've been told I have bats in my throat

Get ready for the night shriek when I puke them up

Another kind of death more spiral than the dust

An ego death where I should start my life

But I don't want any deaths

And I don't want any lives

I want to hunt phantasms in the smeared skies

Give Orion my thighs

Give my blood to the light

Never having been

And so forever born in cosmic leaves

SOURCES OF LIGHT

And the women continued to bleed
They bled what looked like shards of chicken skin
Out their holes
And the men fucked the holes
The good men licked them
It was hard to say who was good
Sometimes when the good men licked
They thought about the next
Bloody hole they would be licking
It was hard to say
But one woman felt sure
The licking of the blood
Meant a man was good
No matter what
So she bound herself to him
And drank of his light
Though there was light in other men
And shining from all kinds of places
Mountains and palm trees and ancient words

Water and sea vegetables

Infinite sources of light

Wherever you turned your eyes it was

If you knew how to see it

And feel it

She felt it

In the mouth of this licking man

Sleep in my light he said

She did

Her blood on his face

Her blood in his light

Pink and then

The vanishing

He had to disappear

As those we make saints of on earth must do

And the light was still inside her

And the light was all around her

But she felt the light go with him

And she prayed she would go too

BIG TIDE

Nothing was made for me

I have to keep making it

Everything was made for me

The ocean, though I didn't know it till I murdered

What evil did I murder that I finally knew the ocean?

No evil no evil I simply saw the ocean

I saw the ocean for the first time

After having seen it for 2000 years

And when I finally saw the ocean

It murdered evil for me

You ask me to define evil

I don't know I can't

I can only say there are things that stand

In the way of other things

And the ocean murders all of them

CADAVER LAMB

When there is no one left

When it is just me and god

What do I say?

I say *help*

I say *freezing*

I say *I am wrong*

But god you never made me feel that way

Humans speak god

I am one of those humans

Many ugly things

Blood head skull hole

Milk mouth teeth rot

Sun hair dick suck

Mother water egg eye

Ugly and real

Ugly and real

I don't want to share

My life with anything real

God is real

I am trying to get better

What does that mean?

WIDE SIGH

I thought that there were two

The good voice

And my voice

I thought the good voice was buried

And I would have to dig

Under my voice

Which is glittery and cold

To get there

Then I heard them

A drumbeat and hawks

Also snakes

Many wild voices

Heartbeats

Big beats

One beat

All over

Do you hear it?

I hear it now

Speeding up

Taking me up

HE SHE

We were kissing in the pigs and fucking in the pigs

My god said it was not love

But my other god said it was

My god just wants me to be happy

And my other god wants me to be happy

And the women have not stopped crying

Throughout history

So I said kill me with your arrow cock

And I will cry too

Only later

LUNAR WIDOW

You will never be a centaur without me

But you will be a gypsy

The stars don't give a shit

We should be under one piece of cloth

Maybe sleep on my hair across the continent

Watch me go up in the sky I do

Now I'm falling into the ocean

You gave me only drops of what I want

I wanted to haul

I wanted to harbor your wreck

Stop not blowing the conch

Be a childhood ok?

The heart so ready before it existed

My mouth on your silence

The dark of not getting what I want

The dark of getting it

Holes forever and ever

Shoes of the father so stepped on

The belly of our thing I don't know what it is

But I know something slit it

Call me a jellyfish

In the evening my body grows a penis

I want you in my odor

And I don't give a shit about the stars

I want your skin for a screen

I can project a cemetery

You can smoke all you want

Welcome to the coffin

AMARANTHINIA

Hi dumb dry memory

You keep hurting my awe

I can hold back till infinity

Then I get to hump the light

I will be so good at infinity

No grey room to frighten me

Only the end of all the stale colors

Everything become all the colors

I used to think I would not live long

Now I think I have my music

And I will become a song when I die

So that even if I die today there is an awesome mercy

Watch me fucking the light

Me licking light from every finger

Me with the light in my ass

Me saying *more* and the light saying *yes*

Me finding out what I always knew

Which is what I know now but cannot remember

I will show the old animals how to be young

This will be my deathless offering

MOON VIOLENCE

The peace I will not pray for

Silence I won't sit in

Zero surrender

The manbaby splayed for my affection

I say no

I ride an animal along the shore

Any animal

I have my knife and money

A throat

I am a woman and no woman at all

The honey drips I taste myself

I eat me in an arc on the water

Dig out my third eye

The hole I fill with sickness this time

Every time

This is what I do with love

REKILLING

Mother nature will forgive me of my killing ways when
    she forgives me
Mother nature will forgive me of my killing ways when
    she kills me
And I don't know if mother nature loves her killings
As I have tried to love my killings
Or if they make her happy
As none have made me happy
Or if the things she kills are beauty
As I kill only beautiful things
Myself mostly
And cruel are the angels who have rescued me
Only to never get inside me
And cruel is the grace that always lived inside me too
    quietly
Cruel eye that brought me to ruin overdosed on humans
Cruel beautiful humans who made the silence seem so
    empty
Both cruel and uncruel is the mystery

So I have had to kill the mystery

I stuffed the mystery up with gyrating statues

Let's lead a spontaneous prayer for the mystery

Please be no void O gyrating mystery

Invoke me and no end of days please mystery

Love me with immaculate feeling zero body

LIQUID ARROWS

Let me give you the gift of dinner

The dinner is mine and it is not mine

It is our dinner and everybody's dinner

There are infinite dinners and there is only one dinner

I will give you the one

I ate at feasts with Bacchus

I ate wild boar and citrons

Brains in rose patina

Cherries, lambs, suckling pig, blood sausages and quinces

The water was cold and the wine seemed nice

Wine was going to be nice for a very long time

Then it would not be nice

I was nine, eleven, thirteen

My breasts came in and there were seven pubic hairs on
    my mound

Bacchus came and laced my cup with serum

A sleeping serum?

No a vomiting serum

In the field I felt that I would vomit

Bacchus sat me on his lap facing the sunset

My legs straddled his knee

The pressure of his knee and the pleasure of the coming
vomit

My seven pubic hairs

The hands of Bacchus clasped around my stomach

My stomach fat but Bacchus didn't care

So my stomach thin

Bacchus put his fingers down my throat to help the vomit
come

I burped and burped but nothing came

I burped like the ocean

I burped like quicksand

Bacchus gave me water to make the vomit come

When I vomited up the water he kept his hand in my
mouth

The vomit went down his arm in a waterfall

The vomit bathed his body

I vomited down his arm all night

The vomit smelled like dead boar

It smelled like brains

It smelled like coins, gladiolus petals, mother's milk and
  cloudrealm

Bacchus said he wanted to hear my stomach scream

I screamed and screamed until I had no more screams

Then I began singing

This was joy

HONEY FIELD

I am an animal outside the church

No I am in the church being good

Incense makes me deep

Like the scorpion under jealousy

Fuck what they say

I can find goodness in a church

I can find it anywhere

So much of my brain is scorching

I have had to learn to find it everywhere

My brain is a jet and purple scorpion

Pacing outside the church

And my heart is the church

It has its bound spire

You know it has its bells and walls

Its plastic love contingency

But in the end dissolve

Like everything infinity

LITTER

My feelings were dogs

With no master left to tend them

But the dogs stayed alive

And discovered they could feed themselves

And I must really love my dogs

Or else I would have stabbed them

So as never to mistake again

A deadbolt for an opening

Because I am a dead girl

And I want to be alive

Though the things that look like life to me

Are somehow a killing

But one day I may get a death

The coming of a kind

That seeks no other death to love

And I'm so scared of choking

DRY FUXX

I dreamt nothing of you tonight because I did not sleep

You were under your hat and I was in my head

I want to be in your head

I am already over

I am widow corpse while soft girls pump wells

They are already over

What if nobody is over?

What if nobody has to end?

I could spit the rain

I could bring the flood

I could say *water water*

I could say this into the nothing

SOFT PALATE

Hear the voice of my hungry bloodhound ghost

She thinks she is a wolf

So full of zeros

Hungry zeros in the hungry bloodhound ghost

Her mother the queen cut out her teeth

To keep her from imaginary destruction

And the hunger ran down her throat

And made an ocean of zeros

But she is tired of that story

Sucking the teeth of other doggies

Damming the ocean with bones

And glittery mirrors and minigods

She goes to the big god

And god is in the ocean

God says *don't drown*

She says *float me*

All the crystals

Of how life is

Some of them

Just look like rocks

ALONG

From the bottom of the ocean come the figures

They are also in the air

Every body we have ever been

Rodents and cheetahs and snakes

You don't have to be anything ever again

You can just be the air

How does it feel with your body gone

Narcissus weeping but the stars like yeah

DOGS

What if the dogs got quiet

And their fur was my hair

And they licked my face

But it was me licking my own face

Also my heart

And the licking built a new kingdom

But the kingdom wasn't in the sky

It was in my hands and on my face

Also in my heart

And I let me be the kindly dogs

And I saw the dogs were always kind

They had only been disguised

Or maybe they were kind and horrible both

Roaming the woods in circles

Until one day they simply walked

Out of the woods

The woods so full of knots

The knots possessing water

The dogs needing every lick of that water

Until they were ready to leave the woods

And when they were finally ready

There was still time

It wasn't sundown

And the dogs looked at the sun

And the sun didn't burn their eyes

And the water in their bellies

And everything outside them

Was all

I RUN RIGHT THROUGH MYSELF
AND DON'T CRACK

The ground under me is nothing

My tendons are nothing

The dick in my palace is nothing

My ancestors eaten by flames are nothing

The flames themselves are something

All my holes are something

Universe universe tell me my secret

The wind in your thoughts and the perfume in your heart

FORGOTTEN SOUND

I pretended the lust was voices

And I wrote down the voices

And sometimes the voices spoke as I had written them

To confirm what I already knew

Which is that I am a child and ready for petting

And sometimes the voices said nothing

To confirm what I already knew

Which is that I am filled with holes

And sometimes the voices said strange words

To confirm what I did not know

Which is that I am a ghost

And the men are real

And going on without me

INSIDE WORLD

Slices of paradise cut in because

Paradise demands our attention

My paradise is a coma I think

It hurts so much to keep walking

Sometimes comas brush against my feet

But I still love on Earth

And will maybe stay alive

Without everything I think I need

The angels are singing me to sleep

The dream of being alive gets born

I get scared and redream it

And everything I touch on Earth

Resembling angels

I try to eat

MAGIC ISN'T DEAD

All the seers predicted who I am

They said *she is a waiting room for bones*

Still I am after some non-predictable end

Where I go beyond skin and hair

I am a fuck demon in a fuck castle

Also electricity and no dust

And I am coming for you spirit

I am avenging everything

The gravestone they tried to make you in the rain

I will make the rain stop

Or I will make it rain animal bodies

And you will see your face in the lions

CHROME COUNTRY

And when you believe you are good

After you have felt wrong for a very long time

The angels come find you and blow in your eyes

And you become a glowing fish

And all of your tears turn to ocean

And the iron world rolls backward

And there in space you are saved

From yourself and also the future

And a quiet voice is all that there is

There in space and floating above it

There in your gills and also your lungs

A quiet voice is all that there is

PROBLEM AREAS

Just don't let me drink from the white tower

Or the grey sane or the black linear

Only the red river

No one knows any more than me

And I am going to have to stay alive

In the mouth of civilization

I ask god to send a swordsman

And god says *look at your hands*

I smell horses on the wind

They are galloping out of my hot lips

LAST SEXT

Am I crying on coal mountain

The sky is a funnel I want it

I want to be sucked by the moon

Or needled into the night

Or into the eye of a cock

Of a boy with a mouth like mine

And together we enter a door in the sky

Which is one door

But all doors

And the breath there is his but mine

And the truth in the door is many

As the truth on coal mountain is many

But also one truth alone

A truth I have felt since always

Before the time of the cock

Do I point to it from my sickbowl

Perched high atop coal mountain

And I can never say its name

As I gape into the dark

And see the jaw of a boy

Reflected in my sickbowl

My bowl of gristle and blood

My thoughts of bellies and scythes

And how to cut me out of me

The vine of the mind and the heart and its sword

And the smoke of the coals in the dark

And his hands on my dress and his mouth on my death

And the bites of want in the dawn

When the boy disappears with the sun

How his body becomes a soot

And his semen dissolves in the wind

But his shadow remains on coal mountain

Am I mine

MERCY FUXX

God wants me to have a lemon tree

Or else I wouldn't have it

And now the horses must come rescue me

Or if no horses, you

Please bring on a stampede

Bring on the fake salvation faster than I could

And I would sodomize with you all evening if I could

Though in the dark

You looked so human in your skin

That I called you human in my head

And did not want you then

And felt relieved

ALONE

I heard the bubblings of a liquid inside

Not plasma or pus or sex wet

An unearthly liquid, so other

And I was told to keep it inside till forever

Now I cry astral tears for all the fake holies

This is how you alchemize you cry

I can teach you alchemy if you lick my astral tears

Or maybe just watch me

LONG TOMB

My pussy tastes like rain to you

I will not make this a romantic poem

Poems are made of mistakes

Poems about poetry are mistakes

I look to mistakes and say *am I ok?*

I look to mistakes and say *make me ok*

My pussy tastes like pussy

And I have been scared since the day I was born

HOW I GET OVER MY LIFE

I turn my mind to bread and feed it to dogs

The dogs are good of stars and never devils

They eat me into something better maybe a door

They eat me to a sky until I'm gone from me

They swallow all my voices cold and drill

They hollow me out for all the good secrets

The secrets give me third eye until sunrise

I shut my mouth the whole time

LAST TERROR

What kind of thing would orphan a mind

Was it the abyss

With its infinite carves

Or the everywhere of graves

That said I was alone

My darling piggie

Darling piggie orphan of my mind

I will unearth you to the snouts of your tribe

Even if we have to leave the Earth

I will find you a home

And forgive you in your slops

Even as you eat my head and hair and heart

I'M COMING

The people talked to me of god

Then god talked to me of god

God said *do not move*

I said *I know*

And then got very still and knew that I was not

And saw our shadows in the room

Two wild and kindly dogs

Leaking light from out their wet jaws

The good of breath from where we all began

Though our minds try to tell a different story

A tale of man and his machete

Murder of our dogs when we fake being men

Or live a lifetime in the human codes

Fierce we cut the shadows with our seeing-eye bones

Gently then we dress the wounds

In nothing

That will lead us back to Earth

Grateful acknowledgment is made to the editors of the
following publications, where some of these poems first
appeared:

POETRY, *Denver Quarterly, Tin House,* Flavorwire, PEN,
Rhizome, Poets.org, *Gigantic, Adult,* Typo, The Volta,
Paperbag, NewHive, *Ping Pong, Third Rail Quarterly,*
Glittermob, *The Atlas Review,* Powder Keg

Much love and gratitude to Meredith Kaffel Simonoff,
Tony Perez, Matthew Dickman, Jakob Vala, Nanci
McCloskey, Meg Cassidy, everyone else behind the scenes
at Tin House, Daniel Lopatin, Dorothea Lasky, Patricia
Lockwood, Zach Verdin, Venice Beach, Pickle, and
always, Nicholas Poluhoff.